The

Journey

Home

WRITTEN AND ILLUSTRATED
BY
A. Nanda

Print ISBN: 978-1-09830-358-7

eBook ISBN: 978-1-09830-359-4

Dedicated to...
all those who take this journey.

CONTENTS

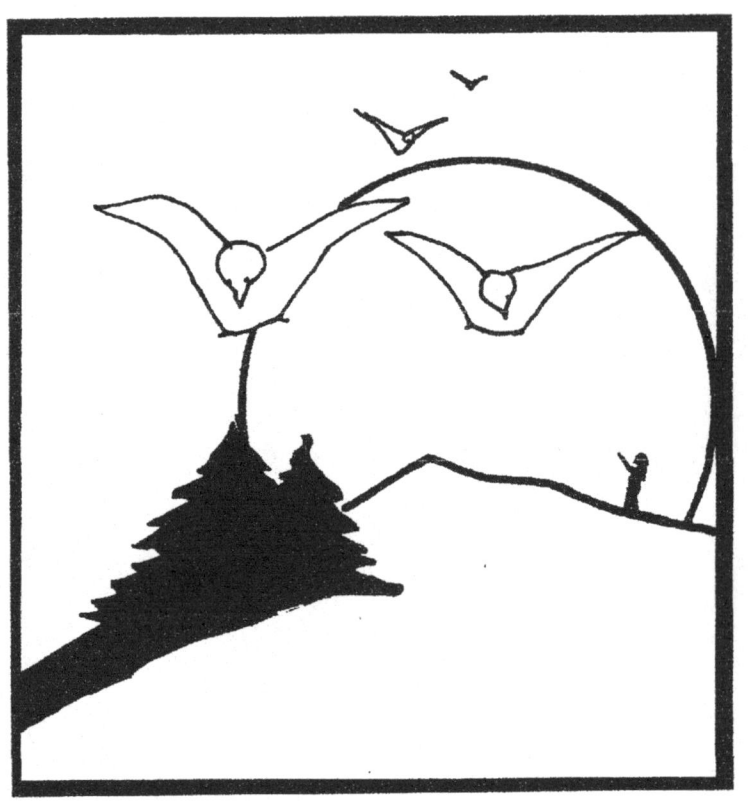

Forward

She threw her arms back and said to the wind,
"Which way do you go? That I may find my way back when I follow?"
The wind did not reply. She followed the wind singing songs to it, all day
into the night. She traveled out of the lush valley where she had begun.

She entered into a new rise of land, with many-a-dip, followed by an
incline. Then, a leveling out. This was a safe level place! Or was it?
It was unfamiliar. She was confused. She continued on, dismissing the
need to rest. She sang to keep up her courage.

The wind blustered as dawn broke. Mist and cold traveled with the wind
now too. The inclines grew steeper, each step wearied her more and
more. Her throat was now too tight and dry to allow for a song.

Day became night once more. There was no moon to lighten her path,
nor stars to guide her, for the mist clung jealously to the ground. Too
weary she had to rest for even her hands hurt from catching near
falls. She shivered with cold. When she sat down to catch her breath,
almost at once she fell asleep.

The next morning the sun awakened her. She blinked the sleep away and
stood up. The mist had gone, the wind was calm. She had slept on the
top of the mountain! There was a worn path up its side. Others had
traveled before her.

Looking down the mountain she could see the highlands. Beyond the
highlands her lush green valley. It was so far off, she had to squint to
focus. From here she could see everything!

She had climbed a mountain to the summit! Smiling up at the sky,
she threw her arms back and turned around and around. She sang to
the sun! She sang with a strong voice, **as the wind stirred ...**

PART ONE

In the Valley

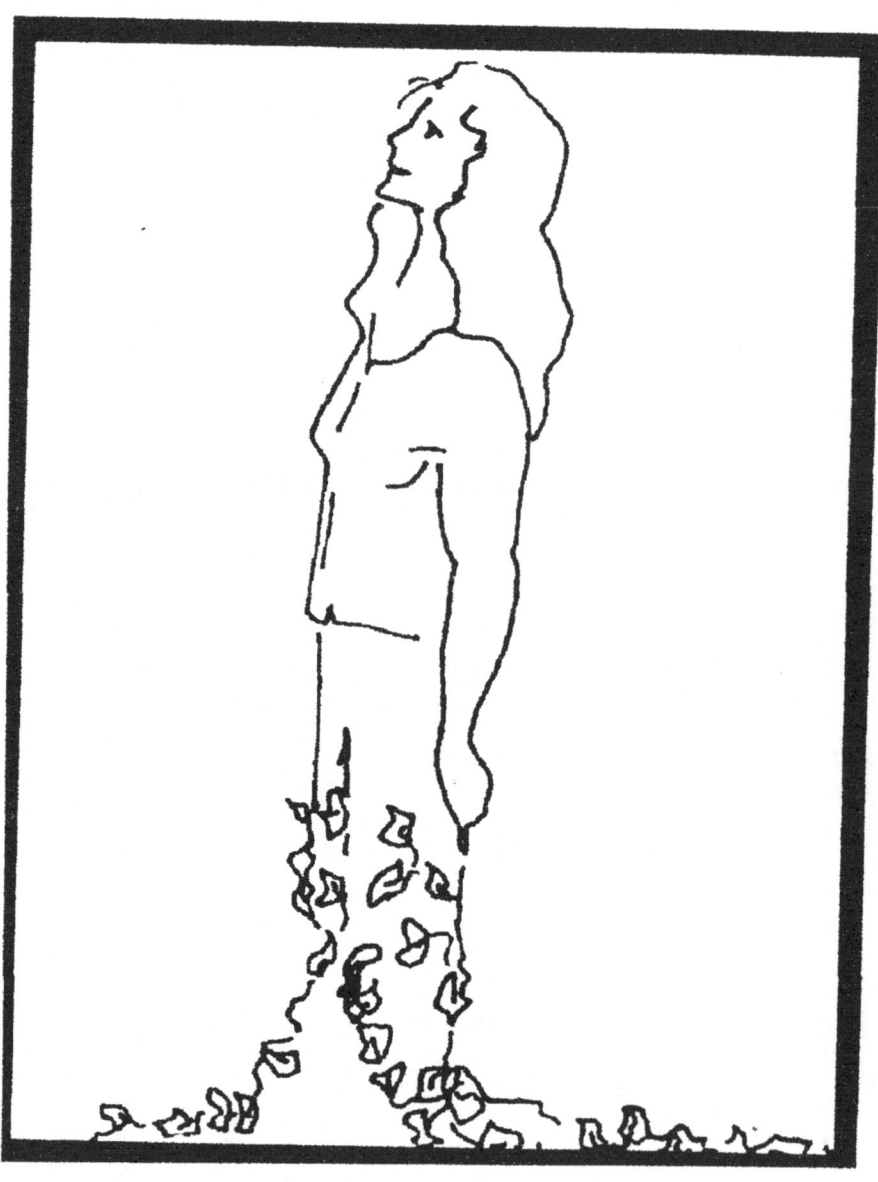

The Land we made

The bright eyes of a God,
The limbs so strong,
The stature that stands alone-
So upright,
The disposition of colors
Balanced and harmonized.

This is you and me - Gods!
We rule the land we made.
Tending our flowers,
plucking out doubt,
The ivy growing 'round our legs.

Caught up
With the dew in the beginning
And torrents by winter pain.

As a child,

I spoke to the flowers and the trees
Begging their forgiveness,
I was so clumsy and so without beauty.

I sometimes weakly, in a whisper,
Cursed the shadow of people forever intruding,
With their

Speeches! Speeches! Speeches!

Soon enough I could turn away
And meet the bright flowers Resting under a cloud
And watch the trees blowing, But the waiting!

The storms,
When they came...
I was outside with the wind and the rain! They were my friends too.

Other children,
Let them have their dead toys! I was alive!
And all the outside became my brother and sister!

I was forever young,
just beginning,
I was a child
Dying of old age!

Tottering Worries

It's a world of tottering worries. It's a
time not to make-believe.
To do-it-now and get-it-done
and face the face you'd rather ignore.

It's a face-it-now, do-it-now world of tottering worries.

It's a world where you can
and sometimes have-no-choice about it. It's an empty headed,
sleepers-walking-about place, and I'm afraid to face it.

Where nobody knows everything,
yet everyone has directions to that end.

But, since there is no end to it.
It's a face-it-now,
worry now,
pay-for-it-later,
I'm sorry-I-got-in-your-way world,
that I should sooner face then run away from

But I like to make-believe!

Surrender

Floating hearts without scars
melting from the sun,
I don't try to stop a thing
I just let it come.

Dressed Like A Clown

Too nervous the air
I can not breathe,
I hoped that you
would feel for me,
but alas, no.

Still the air
though colder now,
has strung up my feelings
dressed them like a clown,
without the laughter
but a sorry frown.

What I saw today

O God! I have to tell you
what I saw today,
I saw a bird fly far away.

And as she flew,
so as she went,
I could see her wings
were bent!

Clear Skies

I do not want to leave
the valley is much
        darker and deeper
           without.

The love is lonely too.
The people false shadows
I have animated myself.

Don't leave!
Don't let me leave!
I must be in you
        and your crystal perception
           in me.

Or else why?

The rain will be around,
clear skies,
just lies...
I put up there.

Boat Rides And Moon Rises

What reason than have I
if boat rides
and moon rises
are all the same?
God is always in another place!

I find the moon round
when I come out,
the water high,
the boats rolling out to sea.

Roll over the oars!
Come inside!
Please! Come in....

Alone

God takes care of the young
and finds homes for some,
others are left out in the wind.

Looking, staring,
afterwards uncaring.

Someday I will die!
And decay
and cheer
"They shall not crush me here!"

For the land without feeling
shall wrack and sway,
devouring me someday!

And Lonely

The man below me
lost his mother,
stands outside his door
and stares.

Lived alone
loved her only,
without her there
he is lonely.

The man above me
and his wife,
lets his mother
share their life.

A Story

The trees were sitting just like before ...
rooted to the ground. Bound not to move anymore,
except for the branches, leaves and fruit.
They were waiting quietly for visitors like you ...

One day there came a gathering of children,
who along side the forest played their games.
Step after step they made their way ...

The trees stand high over their heads,
next to the children the trees look dead!
In the stillest of air the branches stir ...

Down, down move the branches,
a fruit touches a child's chin,
Straight away she starts eating all happily in her head.
Silent and still they all become and soon begin to fall
down one by one ...

The trees dance as best trees can,
while the children lie unconscious on their heads.
Who could know and who would tell,
what that fruit was like just from its smell?
Pink and round with green leaves growing,
but inside hidden away, was that spot of poison
that betrays ...

Who could know?
And who would tell?
If not, of course, the trees themselves.

Paradox

The same soul that lifts me up,
drags me down;
I am number one in the game,
standing at the end.

As I press forward,
I am left behind;
always strong till the end,
weak from the beginning.

Cobwebs clutter the new hallway,
I turn against them;
accepting them at once,
my heritage.

I race forward,
in the times when I walk;
onto a straight path,
turning over on its crooked corners.

What Toll?

The flowers bend down
touching the Earth,
they feel their existence
when nothing is heard.

When the soft petals
are crushed by the rain,
the stem is still standing
so (at least) something remains.

But if I should be crushed
and my figure is still whole,
outwardly standing,
inwardly the toll.

Bells in the Tower

Put your children to sleep, send them back to bed;
for we "other world beings" must have council with them.

Now, as your leader I expect to find no reason nor light of day
in all of their seasons.

After our meeting I went off to see
a large group of Earth children hiding under the trees.

I yelled from the window to all them below,
"that isn't the way to grow gracefully old".

Reflecting on the council there were things left unsaid;
a strategy perhaps? A plan for our death?

As we left the city they rang bells in the tower;
the Earth children thinking we were under their power.

We didn't cry not even a sigh;
we marched homeward in view of the time.

We sat on our boxes, our couches and stools;
and wondered aloud "How they could be so cruel"?

Wondering quietly how could they have planned,
to overthrow this world for a society of man's?

History

To grow
is quite a task;
first at the beginning
nearing last.

Nothing from nothing,
it follows suite;
wind the clock,
sip your soup.

Sit while the sun
goes from east to west;
hope you've flown forward
sideways at best.

But we glimpse the scenes
in acts already done;
and now again
the play has just begun.

Going back is always fun,
to start all over
on the count of one;
"humdrum, humdrum".

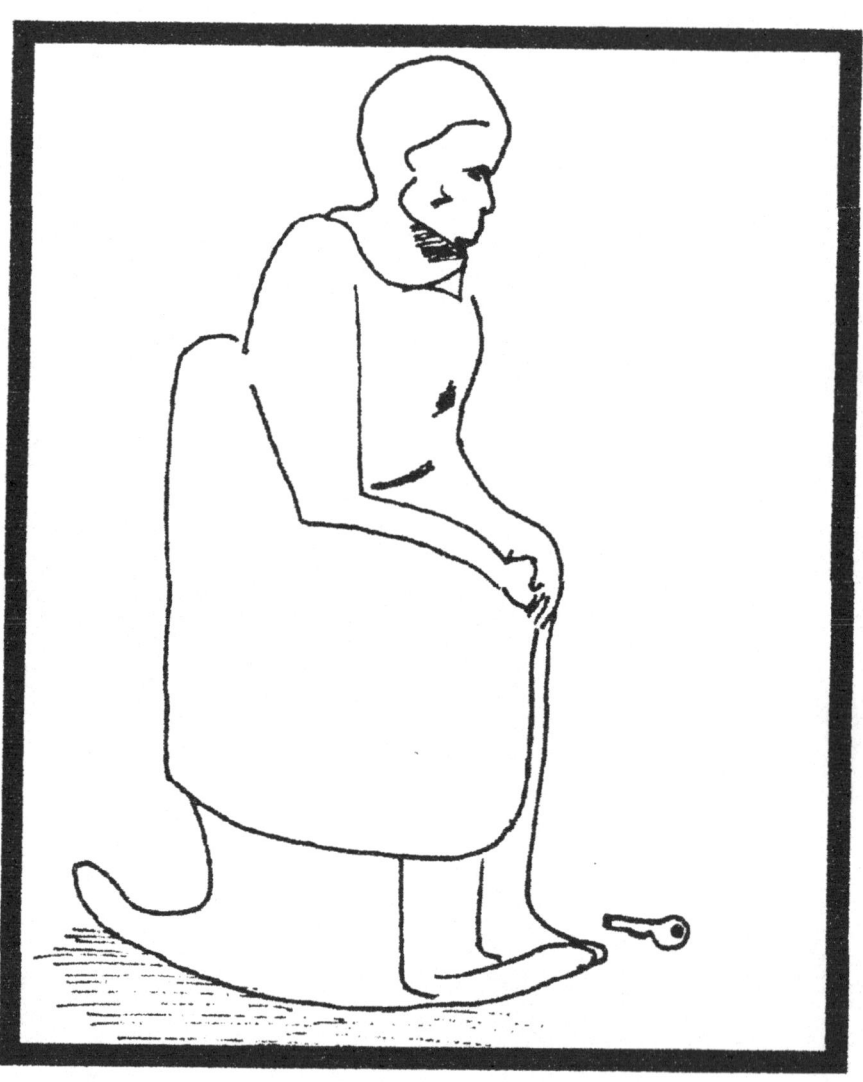

Looking For The Key

I lived at times
within the quiet hour,
shutting those doors tight-locking.

Sat back rocking, very
still, falling into thinking...
which key-like key unlocks
those doors that must?

Did I do it myself?
Can I undo it as well?
With what, where, which-direction key?

For who can look?
Or ask to tell?
And who can unlock it except me, myself?

Disillusioned

The final illusion
has broken at last,
I sit and think
upon the grass....

Covered with fire
fallen from the sun,
my skin was charred
still I was not done.

I could not stop
the death of 'That'
those dreams I collected
in all of my past.

It must be agreed
those flowers I picked,
hid tiny spiders
that cobwebbed me in.

Though this was so
I can not stay,
in a world of appearance
where I only **appear** safe.

Where, Oh Where?

Where should I go
if I shouldn't
stay here?

Among the laughter
and
the tears,

Sitting in the midst
of
a million years,

Where, oh where
should I go
from here?

Some People Know

Singing against the clover
sad songs hit the hills,
windy streets to walk down
silent roads to chance.

Then you meet the sunrise
 and you come to be,
one among the millions
down there where you speak.

When you start to shiver
and there's nowhere to be seen,
just one bush to hide in
down there where you speak.

If your voice starts rising
and you are not heard,
believe that some people know
without the use of words.

PART TWO

Crossing the Highlands

Awaken!

Riding on and on until the sun became warm against her back.

The pink rose and the yellow streaked,

brought her to her beauty as the sun rose so high.

Heaven serenely in the desert now ,

the dry warm heart of God itself.

She rode passed

her horse pearling sweat,

stopping her.

Slowly she chose to lead him into the stream up over his back.

In the songs of Earth,

the herbs she picked before, dried now;

swirling cool water set, tonic for a journey.

Soul travel to awakening.

Mount!

Riding cool as the breeze rushes over her wet now,

farther on...

Another day till evening and morn after;

again day into night on and on

The stars wink,

the swift going,

the leaves waving her on,

encouraging elements as she goes...

Seeking to awaken from illusion!

Seasons In Me

The spring is the flowering-me,
    and the fall is my falling leaves;
How can I blossom and fall
    simultaneously?

The season of growing is tugging at me.
    How can I harvest?
How can the not-fully-grown be
    harvested in me?

About Going On And On for no Reason

I went to the east to sea and
foam of times when soft bushels
of leaves against my back and
the creek lingering by for me.

I met the cold and rushed into
warm and nothing still remains for
I have found no truth.
I think I still feel less too
much for me and can not see
freely into the light. When
shocked and time was strolling
with me not to vanity it
has all turned for I have
decreased since.

You searched the ashes for
me I searched for you by
degrees until I fell over
onto the sides too surely to
remain. Now I can not count
any worth for so much reading
and so many wishing-to-know
looks.

Pondering

Among the trees
long quiet hours of play,
then the noise
as if to say,
its time now
lets go away.

. . . .And we sit
and ponder everything,
listening to the words
silence brings.

You come
in the splendor,
I run
to follow you.
In the fun
your follower now!

. . . .And we sit
and ponder everything,
listening to the words
silence brings.

Watch Your Step

You and I must sit for now
and watch this storm arise;
It's getting hot...it's getting cold.

Cover up, or take off your clothes,
it's time to leave, no, stay at home...
it's getting wet outside.

The storm is here...it's almost gone,
its wet and beginning to dry.
Are we on the brink of another spell?

My heart is rising, ready to fall
and she's depressed
from the joy of it all.

Quiet! Listen! I hear a sound...
Everything is different now,
watch your step or

    you'll

        fall

           down!

Individuality?

The shadow races fast
to meet the evening breeze,
but the light makes it grow dimmer
till it can't even be seen.

The leaves start to fall
they cluster all around
till one becomes another
and they fill the barren ground.

And the one you had your eyes on
has become lost in the sea
and now the growing cluster
kills its individuality.

The bird flying over
sings a song that you must hear
but the flock that's now approaching
makes the sound that was so clear.

Become just another message
to you, a senseless noise,
a chirp of utter confusion
and an indistinctive voice

No Reply

I went on a journey not very far,
to get rid of the grief that locks me in bars.

My memories hidden in my pockets
I was going away to hock them,
far from remembrances and deep reminders.

I walked, no I ran down to this land,
it was sunken and deep.
They told me my memories would,
                "Sleep, sleep".

Well, I exchanged those pains
till nothing remained,
I hocked them to a pair of visionaries.

Now as I walked away
                I said,
                "Feeling like an empty bag,
                nothing to shoulder
                nothing to drag-me-down."

When coming up from this land
hidden in the deep,
all-of- a-sudden I began to weep.

... I could not remember,
and would I ever know why?
My mind was silent, there was no reply.

I exchanged my pains for forgetfulness,
and now must live without,
access to healing memories
... of my dreams of God.

Falling Down

The tower is falling
I see it tumbling down,
and all that stand beneath it
are immediately wiped out.

The tower was their joy
it came for just one time,
to see if they could know it
and understand its rhyme.

That rhyme is speaking softly
it tells of the time,
when it could come and go
and be neither yours nor mine.

Together

The pale round orb in the sky
    shines in your eyes
    under the dark night sky
        of my dreams.
And I see your rounded nose
    and your long relaxed pose,
    against the tree trunk
        of time.

I sweep from a far away carriage
    led in a noc-eternal marriage,
    reconfirming our youthful
        affirmation of love.
Riding on wheels hidden under
    backgrounds of soft thunder,
    ringing the seasons of
        a big fat year.

The old fear of losing ground
    is again in dreaming found,
    but our houses are reaching out
        bravely together.

Directions

I stood in the midst of the highlands
looking at the roads that lead away;
if it hadn't been for your directions
I 'd still be standing there right to this day.

Since I'm now on the road **to where** I'm **going**
I can easily see that there's no end;
But, if I leave off my going
I'll never even reach the bend!

PART THREE

On the Mountain

Reflections

I am not in the village anymore,
I've left it behind.
All the pruned trees and stone steps,
the curved roads and cottages,
the wisps of smoke from evening fires
are below me now.
Like a toy landscape;
far away and small.
I'm dispassionate about it.

I am somewhere on the mountain,
but I don't know where.
I have no map or compass,
just memories of teachings.

I don't know when or how I got here.
Maybe it was all the effort I put out?
Or maybe it was from all the longing?

I only realized I was here on reflection.
When I wondered why I didn't feel the same about so many things.

Then, the sudden knowing appeared.
It told me I had left my little village
and was now on the mountain.
Just that knowing has changed me.

Tonight, the moon is small, the forest dark,
and I am somewhere on the mountain...
looking intently,
listening to all the sounds.

Looking...

I am looking for God in the field

...I have found just a little so far.

The animals are twisting, red yellow and soft blue,

chasing me into lines and out of monotonous indifference.

Because it is timeless light coming and going around.

on and off the Earth world surface.

I am looking for God in the ocean

...and in the lights and shadows of it all The Divine is swimming.

Gypsies are driving herds of mystics through Sacred Hands

and Those Feet are standing on me.

I am looking for God in the hills

...among the oak and madrone.

The sacred is all I have ever known.

I have much to learn to ease my mind,

and I have counted a million years to my search.

I am looking for God in the village

...and my senses have become confused,

my time is going to waste with idle words.

I have found but a little so far...

like the timeless light it comes and goes around,

on and off the Earth world surface.

The World Is Round

We have built our homes on separate continents;
moving even further apart
by our crazy logic.
Pushing the Earth below us,
easing our boats away...away...away.

Until, we have grown so far apart
that we have touched again,
on the other side of the world.
Sides opposite,
that we did not guard against.

Only proves to us,
the world is round!
And the further we go away,
the closer we come together.
No longer waving handkerchiefs from aways;
save,
protected,
alone!

We are so close now,
I merely jump a seeming-stream of salt water,
and I am upon you...
like your other hand is to your other hand.

Dear Crystal;

Have I told you,
how your shape has stood
before me,
like something suspended?

Each part of that part
moving slower,
than was really you?
Like a cloud...
dropped into liquid.
It is you Crystalline!

Come here!
I want to feel your form;
One minute different
from tomorrow's
bird or leaf.
Somewhere within or around me?
Crystallized!?

A part of myself perhaps?
Or a cocoon
left behind?

Another View

We took our hands
in clasped fashion,
by way of a murky river
with brown leaves afloat;

You slid into the swamp
under shining cloud,
cool bubbles surfacing
breathing through a reed.

You picked a lilly and a leaf,
placing in my palms,
an idea colored by you,
enlarging my view;

When you fell from the tree,
I was happy to see,
you stood up again
my same whole friend.

Free To Be

The big lonely condor
has an illustrious past,
but she'll surely turn to salt
if she dare look back.

She roamed the north pole
away from all the towns,
she flew the far-away coldness
with her wings held weakly out.

She fed on the cattle
the steers and the cows,
and the children at a fair
running aimlessly around.

Now she hovers over
like an ancient Going-To-Die,
free to be old and fading
free to be in the warmer climes.

A World In Love

The maid stood near the water naked were her feet,

soaked in salt sea water dried by summer's heat.

She walked around the water's edge until she began to tire,

she slept among the sea water rocks safe from the morning sun's fire.

She didn't cry when she was awakened by a terrible gusty wind,

she merely pulled her dress down around and tried to be friends with it.

She put on her prettiest voice the one that sounded so sweet,

and began to tell the wind of how she loved it at her feet.

The wind was overjoyed at once to hear the maiden talk,

it had not heard a compliment since time began on clock.

All day it played around her feet and cooled her from the sun,

frolicking in open spaces, languishing where there were none.

The wind went on its journeys into the hemispheres,

and from the good the maiden brought the wind left better everywhere.

And oh, the hemispheres were glad to see the wind this way,

for the first time since blowing up it blew on down their way.

From the goodness of the wind the hemispheres decided,

that they would not be separated so they became united.

Soon all that lived upon the world gave happiness back and forth,

giving gifts one to another like receiving them from themselves.

So for one brief moment shared all the world felt good inside,

and **it all came back to the maiden** who did little more than **TRY!**

Separate Beings

Come here!
Please sing to me
and answer me in a song;

What eyes would
this darkness see?
And call it light?

Or, where behold
a universe
of **s-e-p-a-r-a-t-e** beings?
Saying **allareone**?

Sing light as a flute
carrying notes,
to the arch
in a universal dome
...then come to me again!

Laughing

I laughed
at dark children,

Bogged down in the river
mud,

Sunk down to their knees
in the shallow end;

I laughed
as they struggled to be
free,

Twisting this way then
back again,

And at myself reflected
in them.

Forever Looks Back

I would turn aside
and follow love down...
The road would lead
and turn
then no more;

At the end
would be the clouds,
the 'Mansions of All';
an endless love affair,
a star-lit night
t that never ends!

"Peace"
shall line my love gown
as forever looks back
through the mirror.

The End